# NEVER AGREE TO SPLIT
# THE BILLS 50/50

ROOMMATES

# NEVER AGREE TO SPLIT THE BILLS 50/50

~~ROOMMATES~~

*A Women's Guide To Attracting And Marrying A Man Who Provides.*

By Ann-Marie Graham

# TABLE OF CONTENTS

# INTRODUCTION

Dear Ladies,

My name is Ann-Marie Graham, but you can call me Dreamer. Welcome to *"Never Agree to Split the Bills 50/50."* You can consider this your guide to marrying a man who Leads, Protects, and Provides. It's high time you stop wearing the pants in the relationship. You are God's Daughter. Why should you settle for less when God provides so much more? It's time for you to start seeing yourself for the queen that you are.

In this book, I will share my mistakes in the dating world as well as pray that you never make them.

We have busy lives in today's modern world with plenty of things to do, places to go, and people to meet. Now is not the time to keep on repeating history. Now is the time to take the throne. It's Elevation Time Beloved!!!

Consider gifting this book to a daughter, a friend, or a sister. If you need one and one coaching, visit www.upfromthedust.org and send us an email.

# CHAPTER ONE

# KNOW YOUR WORTH

The wind was slightly wispy with a touch of sea salt mixed in the air. The perfect day in paradise where dreams are made. It was also my wedding day. I remember perfectly the emotions running through me. I was excited to be getting married, yet oddly enough having a tightness in my belly full of conflict knowing I was accepting significantly less than I deserved.

As I walked up the stairs to the reception hall, I overheard my then uncle-in-law saying, "If this girl was my daughter, she could have never gotten married to this boy today." He was saying if I were his daughter, this wedding would have never taken place because I was worthy of so much more.

It turns out what I heard was a harbinger of bad things to come. Nothing went as planned. Responsibilities were neglected and some people did not contribute their part. I wanted to dance to country music at my wedding but my hubby's job was to prepare the music and there was no band or DJ in sight. Ultimately, do I share a portion of the blame? Yes. The truth is I got married to him that day because I didn't know my worth.

I lacked my father's presence when I was growing up. He wasn't around to affirm me or speak life in me. He wasn't there to teach me how a man is supposed to treat a woman. I didn't expect anything, and I didn't get anything. I didn't get anything because I didn't value myself.

Ladies, I know many of you grew up just like me in a single-family home. Some of you are suffering from low self-esteem. You look good on the outside, but deep down, you are empty. Deep down, you feel like trash. Deep down, you feel like the Becky's of this world deserve good and not you. You feel like those girls who come from good homes deserve the good man and not us. I want you to know that your story changes today. If you are willing to take this journey to marry a good man seriously, you will find and marry your prince. The wrong man can cut your destiny short and affect your future generation.

Ladies allow me to tell you who you are.

## YOU ARE WORTHY

Ladies, you are priceless. Your beauty is not just on the outside. Beauty also comes from within. You are a treasure far more valuable than diamonds and pearls. You are one of a kind. Extraordinary because there is no one like you. You are precious, and you have a whole lot to offer to this world, to your husband, and your future family. Even if you don't have a Ph.D. and live in some mansion in California, you are still valuable. Don't allow little boys to make you feel less than the queen you are. You have a lot to offer by simply being you. As women, we bring a lot to the table: love, class, wisdom, prayer, support, beauty, intelligence, value, encouragement, vision, and purpose.

Now you may be wondering why this chapter is in a book about marrying a man who provides. Well, it has everything to do with it. If you do not know your worth, you will keep on dating boys, losers, and time-wasters.

Poor self-worth will keep the most beautiful woman trapped in a toxic relationship. Not knowing your worth will sabotage new relationships. In a worst-case scenario, a lack of worth may cause you to end up in the hospital with a mental breakdown after a relationship ends. No one is immune from this, celebrities, politicians, and the wealthy alike. Anxiety and depression after a breakup can trigger a mental illness you did not have before. I am not here to sugarcoat my words when your life is at stake. I am here to tell you the truth. The truth sometimes hurts, but I guarantee you this, it will set you free.

Knowing your worth will equip you with the tools you need to Identify what you want out of life and out of a relationship. It will help you to know what you deserve, thus giving you the power to walk away from links that don't lead you to your best self. Finally, knowing your worth can help you to walk away from dead-end relationships and into an incredibly amazing one.

You should never have to change who you are for any man. You shouldn't have to sacrifice the person you were created to be just so that a man can accept you. Even if you are a bit eccentric, you can still find love. The Right man for you will love you flaws and all. No one is perfect; we are all a work in progress. Feel comfortable in your skin, appreciate yourself, and your rightful life partner will do the same.

## IT IS DIFFICULT TO RECEIVE LOVE IF WE DON'T LOVE OURSELVES.

# CHAPTER TWO

# YOU ARE THE PRIZE

*The man who finds a wife finds a treasure, and he receives favor from the LORD.* Proverbs 18:22

Even if you are not a Christian or set a foot in a church, you should consider taking the above scripture to heart. Why? Because this scripture here will determine if you marry a good man or not. Ladies, if you get nothing else from this book, please grab hold of this truth. **"You are a prize to be earned, a treasure to be discovered."**

Let me share a little snippet of another relationship I had. From day one, I doubt I could have called it a relationship. It hurts me to even talk about it. After talking for some time, he still couldn't define the relationship. Of course he didn't see it as a big deal. I had to beg him to set it. That was the first red flag there, but I kept on pursuing him.

We lived in different places, so there you go, it was a long-distance relationship, and this went on for years. We spoke daily on the phone, but each time I ended the call, I was as empty if not more so than when I first went on. Our relationship had no depth or vision. We spoke of nothing concerning the future. Whenever I wanted to talk about certain things, I was told that I was being too pushy and wanted to rush life. Mind you; this was after years of being in the relationship and not even as much as looking at another man. I loved this person with all my heart. My family loved him; my friends loved him for me up until the point where they saw that I was hurting very much.

I prayed; this man wasn't bad. I see where we could do well together and accomplish a lot together, but all that meant very little because this man couldn't commit to me. If he were writing this book, he would have probably said, in life, people should go with the flow, it wasn't time, he has a lot on his plate. He needs to be sure this is what God wants him to do. What if it wasn't God's will. I am just assuming that all those would have been some of his excuses. I stayed in the relationship because I thought in my heart that one day he would grow up and realize that I am a good woman.

I remember a friend of mine who was in a horrible first marriage like myself. Both of our marriages lasted for less than a year, and though I remained single much longer than her, I guess she learned a fundamental lesson that I didn't. She discovered that she is the Prize.

I remember sharing information about my relationship with her, and she said, "Ann-Marie, lay it all down. Give it to God completely.

A man who loves you will run after you. God loves you too much not to grant you a man who is willing to run after you." Years later, my friend is happily married to a wonderful man. When she met her husband, he pursued her and treated her like the Prize and still does even today.

My friend discovered that she is this Prize, I finally came to my senses, and its full time for you to do the same, my friend.

Ladies, I am going to tell you the same thing my friend told me and a bit more. Never pursue a man, if he genuinely loves you, he will pursue you. You won't have to beg him to define the relationship or ask him to introduce you to family. You won't have to give him hints to propose to you or set a wedding date. He will pursue, he will lead. He won't play games. You won't be the one always driving to his house or setting up weekend encounters. He will plan for the long term with you and not just the weekends.

The man who sees, acknowledges, and values you as the Prize will be intentional. He will make it clear that you are the Prize. He will make plans for the future and not just for summer.

Ladies, the moment you start pursuing a man, you have automatically made him the Prize. And if he is the Prize, what are you? I was thirsty for a man and a husband. I didn't want to sleep alone another night; after all, I spend most of my life being alone. I was exhibiting the attitude of a thirsty woman. I was hungry, unsure of my worth, and I attracted men who were enticed by these kinds of women.

Ladies, it's time for you to raise the bar. Raise your vibration. You are the Prize. You are the Treasure. He who finds a wife finds a good thing. Stop pursuing him and let him court you. If you are guilty of this kind of behavior, decide to stop today and turn it over to God completely. You deserve a man who will treat and value you as the Treasure that you are.

# CHAPTER THREE

## LISTEN TO WHAT GRANDMA TOLD YOU

A conversation I had with my grandma several years after my first marriage ended. (Affectionately she called me Crystal)

Crystal: "Grandma, I have been praying for a husband. I want to find a man that I love so much. I want to get married, and I want to have children."

Grandma begins to lecture me in her old age: "So you are telling me that you want to find the man, and you want to marry for love? First of all, you don't find the man; the man finds and pursues you. This is the problem with young women of today. Crystal, listen to me; you marry for love once, right? Where did it get you?"

Crystal: "What do you mean, Grandma? What are you trying to get across? Yes, I got married for love, and I will fall in love and get married again."

Grandma: "I am not saying love isn't necessary because it is, but when I met Sylvan (her husband), I was young, my parents were dead, and I had to provide for my younger siblings. Sylvan loved me, and he provided for me that way I could provide for my family. I didn't fall in love with him overnight like you young people do today. I grew in love with him because of how he treated me, and that is the reason why we stayed married until death separated us."

Crystal: "He was a good man, and I am happy it worked out well for you. God knows if it weren't for him, my mom and I wouldn't have had a home. He had a big and kind heart and is still my favorite person, even in death." (My mom was adopted that was how they both became my grandparents.)

Grandma: "It's time to be smart, Crystal, soon I won't be here to tell you this. Marry a man who loves you more than you love him. The man who loves you more will do anything for you. Marry for stability and protection. You are getting older, marry a man who can take care of you and those children you want to have one day. Don't be stupid. Go pray and ask God to lead you and get out of my face with your nonsense."

Crystal: "No, Grandma, not me. I don't care if the man doesn't have a penny to his name. If I love him, I will marry him. I must feel something in my heart. I love love."

Grandma: "When hungry comes through the front door, love goes through the back door. One day you will understand."

So that was a conversation I had with my grandma about two years before she went on to be with the Lord. She got into a relationship with my grandpa when she was sixteen, and he was a little older. They were married up until February of 2013 when my grandfather died at the age of ninety, and she died six years later.

After so many years, I finally understand that conversation between my grandma and I. She had enormous ideas on how a relationship and a marriage should work. She would lecture anyone and everyone on the fact that a man should Lead, Protect, and Provide for his family. She said this was their God-given duty, and a real man will respect and value such a sacred responsibility. I delve further on this in another chapter, but right now, I want to focus on the issue of stability.

Ladies, most of us had terrific grandparents who taught us to marry a solid man. One who can lead, protect, and provide. Truth is, a lot of us don't listen to our grandparents, we listen to our angry mothers who didn't listen to their parents and had to learn the hard way.

Ladies here are some facts that very few of you know about, People who marry for love only rarely have long and healthy marriages. People who marry for procreation, financial security, and companionship have longer and better marriages.

The reason for that is because they didn't get married based on some butterfly feelings; they got married for a purpose. I choose to use the word butterfly feelings in this context because the truth is, most people only know about the butterfly feelings. We don't know genuine unconditional love, which is eighty percent choice and twenty percent feelings. My grandparents had real love; they grew into it.

Ladies, I know how difficult it is when you tell your friends that you can't marry for love alone. Everyone doesn't want to hear that. The moment that sentence comes out of your mouth, small-minded people label you as a gold digger. Sweetie, you are not a gold digger; you are a Goal Digger. And when you are Digging for Goals, trust me, some gold is involved as well.

I bet your grandma wouldn't consider you manipulative if you told her you needed more than love to get married. I bet she would probably get a wine glass, pour you a glass of wine, and celebrate the fact that her granddaughter is elevating herself.

In the Victorian Era, divorce was rare. People back then seldom got married for love. They got married for a higher purpose. We are now in the twenty-first century, and people are getting out of marriages as fast as they got in.

When you marry for purpose, the expectation of your marriage and your husband becomes a realistic one. You understand that your husband is a man with flaws, just like you are a woman with flaws. My grandpa wasn't perfect, He wasn't The One like so many romantics would call it today, but he was a good enough man who leads, protected and provided for his family the best way he knew how.

Ladies, I am not telling you what to do, but love alone doesn't cut it. Many say they love, but then there are no actions behind their words. You need a man who will put his money where his mouth is.

Before you say Yes to that man, ask yourself

*IS HE A LEADER?*

*IS HE A PROTECTOR?*

*IS HE A PROVIDER?*

If he doesn't, you have no business getting married to him. Boys will call you a gold digger, but there are so many real men in this world waiting to meet, know, and marry a feminine woman like yourself. Listen to your grandma; her advice will save you a lifetime of trouble.

# CHAPTER FOUR

# FORGET WHAT MOMMY SAID

Ladies, I am not saying you shouldn't listen to your mother at all because some of us have great moms in healthy relations with the opposite sex. This chapter is for women who had mothers in very toxic relationships with guys. Mothers who had relationships that weren't life-giving generally tell their daughters that all men are the same. This type of thinking forms a limiting belief in the mind of the adult daughter and thus affects her love life.

A familiar term I hear from women with broken mothers is that all men are the same. Upon careful investigation, I typically discover that this belief later on in life became their actuality. Ladies, the first thing I want to adjust is your mindset. Change your mindset, change your life. If you continue to hold that all men are the same, you will continue to attract the dusty men your mother dated. And you, my friend, you will continue to get into a new relationship with a different low-quality man every few years.

The law of attraction helps us to realize that we don't just attract who we want; we also attract who we are. We invite who we are into our lives based on our vibrational charge. The Bible, as well as the law of attraction, states that man becomes what man thinks about the most. If you are holding negative and limiting beliefs within, then you are a cynical person. What this means is that you and these dusty men are on the same frequency. You are both on the same vibration, the same wavelength, and therefore you attract each other. So change your mindset, change your life. All men aren't the same. As of today, tell yourself that you are a good quality woman, and you are a magnet for a good quality man. Tell yourself each night that good quality men are attracted to you.

Heal that place of internal brokenness that is attracting these types of men. One lady, I knew, kept on entering new relationships. When I carefully examined her life, I encouraged her to see that she was really dating the same man, albeit with a different body and a different name. Perhaps differing physical features but always the same mindset and characteristics. Upon an even closer look, I realized that these men she was dating were exactly like her father. The same man her mother dated. Talk about dysfunction traveling from one generation to the next; this is a common phenomenon. Ladies, we have to emancipate ourselves from what our mothers may have taught us. Construct new beliefs and heal the place of brokenness within us.

Brokenness likes dysfunction. We have to stop attracting dysfunction. Victims attract abusers. Narcissists are attracted to broken people. Women who don't value themselves are generally attracted to men who are none providers. Men who don't love to protect are attracted to masculine women because they want someone to take care of them. To get better, we have to become better, and that starts by taking care of number one. Sometimes healing will require a life coach or a professional counselor. Don't be afraid to get help.

Last but certainly not least, please know that the man you are most attracted to may not always be the man in your best interest. If you keep dating feminine, dusty men and it doesn't work out, upgrade yourself and get yourself a good quality man. If you were going for men who go to the strip club, change your preference and go for a man who plays gulf. If you were going for the most handsome in the room, change your type and go for the average guy with a proper mindset. It is better to have an average gentleman who will love and treat you like a queen than to be with a handsome novice. Ladies, you can change your preference but never downgrade your standard. Do not settle!

# CHAPTER FIVE

# STRONG BLACK WOMAN DOESN'T EXIST

Strong black women, many women of color, jump with joy when they hear these words, but deeply embedded in this stereotype is a trap, a weapon that dehumanizes black women. Young girls grow up, and instead of viewing themselves as a prize and a treasure, they see themselves as a strong black woman. In some cultures, White and Asian women for ages have welcomed the idea of having a husband, a helpmate. It pains my heart to see my black sisters wearing this crown with such honor when it is putting to shame our very existence as a feminine woman.

So who is the strong black woman? A woman who doesn't want a man. A woman who doesn't show her emotions. A woman who can carry a substantial load and an oppressive burden. A masculine woman with a sharp tongue is also regarded as a strong black woman.

Strong black women use to be women who dig and plant. In most recent years, they are the college-educated career women who struggle with loneliness. She looks like wonder women on the outside, doing everything all by herself. Sometimes she does end up getting married, but ninety-nine percent of the time, she ends up being with a feminine man who doesn't value her. A man who does not lead, protect, and provide for her because she is the strong, black woman.

The strong black woman is a stereotype that came from the days of slavery. While the master was in his plantation home, pleased with his wife and children, a family that he did everything to protect, provide, and lead. The strong black women were out in the cotton field in the rain, picking cotton and plowing the land.

She wasn't allowed to get married, and the male slaves she occasionally slept with were beaten right before her very eyes time and time again. Children she gave birth to were ripped from her bosom. A woman like this had no option but to be tough and masculine. It was needed to survive; she didn't have the luxury to relax and enjoy life. Now we are in the Twenty-First Century, and so many black sisters are still caught in mental slavery holding on to a title that was placed upon them by people who saw them as less than human. And the black men, a lot of them are still in slavery and refuse to rise to the occasion to be leaders, protectors, and providers for their family.

Today the same pattern follows, the strong black woman is a single mother with four children. She is a woman who is stuck on welfare in the ghettos of the world. And if this isn't the case, she is a successful overbearing woman who is with a dusty.

Ladies, I know that many of us got this survival instinct from our mothers, but it is our responsibility to let this limiting belief go and develop a new consciousness. If we look in society today, we will see

NEVER AGREE TO SPLIT THE BILLS 50/50

thousands and thousands of girls who left high school, went to college, got married, and start a family, never worked a day in her life. When asked her occupation, she will proudly say she is a stay at home wife and mom. She proudly tells this to her friends and anyone she happens to meet. People prize her and celebrate her. In certain circles, a black woman does this, and society calls her lazy.

I am not telling you that this is what you should or should not do with your life. I am merely saying you should have the choice if this is what you want and desire. Another young woman I knew was twenty-eight and never worked a day in her life. I would often encourage her to find something to do, pursue purpose, and make something of herself. One day she told me she didn't feel called to work outside the home as she was destined to become a wife and a mother. She never worked a day in her life, and today she is a stay at home wife, happily married. Her husband leads, protect, and provides for her.

I am not teaching girls to get sugar daddies or anything like that or even play silly games. I am encouraging women to think about their future and make wholesome decisions because this is God's best for them.

Many black women today are dealing with a lot of stress, emotional turmoil, and numbness. We have bottled up our emotions inside for years. We are putting everyone first but ourselves, forgetting our own needs and wants, not believing that we deserve help. Black woman has given love and support; she has sacrificed much without expecting anything in return. Black woman, it's time for you to start expecting something.

We are told not to show our emotions or ask for help, if we do that we are seen as weak.

Black women give me the opportunity to speak life into you. You are the essence of femininity; you are desirable; you are beautiful. Your King will find you, and he will lead, protect, and provide for you. You don't have to settle for a dusty. Your strong man is coming. He is out there, and he is attracted to your beauty. He knows that you have a lot to offer him, and he has a lot to provide. He will be impressed by your ideals, and you will be attracted to his character. He won't try to change you or make you into a strong black woman; you will be his compliment.

Let go of the strong black woman stereotype type. It keeps you alone and single. It's keeping you in poverty trying to make life with a dusty man who offers you nothing but pain and more pain.

You deserve the Princess Experience.

# CHAPTER SIX

# WAKE UP AND SMELL THE COFFEE

Why buy the cow when you can milk it for free? This idiom doesn't just apply to sex; it applies to other things as well. We, as women, need to know that it is not official until it is official. "Wake up and smell the coffee" is your guide to not giving away the milk for free. Don't treat your boyfriend like a husband when he isn't. Doing that is keeping you single for much longer, and it also shows that you don't know your worth.

I use to know a young man in his early twenties when I lived with my mom. Every few months, he would bring a different girl home. Sadly, all these girls thought they were the woman of his dreams. They would move into his house, wash, cook, and clean for him. They all treated him like a king. Though I wasn't in their bedroom, I am pretty sure they were having sexual intercourse.

My mother and I would talk about it each time a new girl came. Sometimes he would break up with them and tell them to leave his house, and at other times they would get frustrated and leave. This lifestyle went on for years. A common complaint among the girls was that they were working in the home, taking care of this young man, and yet he couldn't even give them money to do their hair or buy a change of garment. He was extremely stingy, and he was not motivated to change and do better because he was already getting everything for free. All these girls treated him like a husband though it was clear that he was just a boyfriend.

Many women begin treating their boyfriends like a husband from the very moment they define their relationship. A select few even start treating him like a husband before the connection is established in hopes that he will define it and take it further. Ladies, I don't know if you have done this in the past or if you are currently doing this, but it is not okay. Unless that man brings you before a pastor or to the courthouse and you guys are legally married, he is not your husband. And legally, you are single! Been dating for ten years? You are still single in the eyes of the law.

## PLAYING HOUSE

The longest I have ever stayed at a man's house who I wasn't married to is two months, and trust me, that was way too long. While being there, I realized the adverse effects this can have on one's emotions. Playing house is not cool. It may help you to feel a bit closer to your boyfriend, but in the end, it's just an illusion. Living together can feel like a marriage, but it doesn't carry the foundation, the comfort, and security of a real marriage.

While playing house, you are more than likely giving him sex, cooking for him, doing his laundry, providing a breast for him to lay his head on at nights, rubbing his feet, rubbing his head, providing a safe haven for him to release himself emotionally and even spiritually. You can do all that, and he can wake up one morning and tell you to leave or replace you with another girl. The sad thing is some women have done this for years, and as soon as they are a bit older, men have traded them in for a younger version.

Now when a man tells a woman the relationship is over, a woman who has spent years playing wife is usually the one disappointed. All the man will say is, "she was such a good woman." You don't want to be called just a good woman; you are the prize and should be treated as such. It's time for you to know your worth and stop treating boyfriends like husbands.

The benefits of marriage don't apply to a boyfriend or girlfriend relationship. It doesn't even apply if you guys are engaged. If you go to the doctor's office, to the bank or some government institution, you can't put down that you are married. You are single! Now, if you are single in the eyes of God and the eyes of the law, why should you be giving him husband benefits when he isn't married to you.

Treating a man like a husband before marriage will keep you in the singles club. I was watching an online video platform and came across a young lady crying her eyes out. She dated a man for seven years; she lived with him, cooked for him, and did everything a wife did. Each time this man promised her marriage, but it never materialized. At one point, he even proposed to her but wouldn't set a wedding date. After several years of this madness, she came to her senses and moved out. She was tired of treating this man like a husband who was never going to make her a wife. Six months later, this same man got married to another who didn't live with him or do all that his former girlfriend did. It broke my heart hearing the story because I could tell that the girl who was playing house is a good woman. She was a good woman who didn't see herself as the treasure.

I am not telling you not to date, but I believe courting is so much better. Courting is the experience of establishing an intense spiritual and emotional relationship with the desire to see if marriage is the correct choice. God is at the center of this relationship. Courtship is to be accomplished without the complexity of sexual intimacy. This way, the couple has plenty of time to learn about each other, build trust, and foster unconditional love. Most importantly, courtships are never to be dragged out; they are intentional. Sometimes they are broken off, but at least everyone walks away with their integrity still intact.

Now I do understand that it is good to get to know each other, and that takes time, but if your boyfriend wants to be treated like a husband, he needs to do the right thing and make it official. He needs to show you that he wants you to become family. He does this by asking you to marry him and following through with it.

Ladies be suspicious of men who propose but who can never set a wedding date. This is an old trick in the book. Our above sister fell for it and stayed in a dead-end relationship for seven years waiting for a wedding day that never came. Don't allow an engagement ring to turn black and moldy on your finger while waiting for happily ever after. A lot of men want the benefits of a wife without committing.

CHAPTER SEVEN

# SAY GOODBYE TO MAMA'S BOY

*Therefore shall a man leave his father and his mother and shall cleave unto his wife: and they shall be one flesh.*
Genesis 2:24 KJV

Dear future wives, this scripture gives a clear pattern of marriage, one that a mama's boy can't fulfill. In this scripture, God reveals his plan for marriage, in that a man must leave or forsake his parents and stick to his wife. For a man and woman to become one, leaving and cleaving is an important step not to be taken lightly. God designed marriage because he didn't want the man to be alone. When you get married, your husband becomes your companion and vice versa. A new family unit is formed.

When the bible talks about a man leaving his parents and cleaving to his wife, it means a transfer of loyalty and allegiance. It means that the wife should now become his number one priority and not his parents. Leading, protecting and providing for his wife should be his number one goal.

Ladies, I make no apologies when I say this, but a mama's boy can't provide you with that. My desire is for you to marry a real man. STAY AWAY FROM THE MAMA'S BOY! The very name makes me feel like I want to barf. There is nothing sexy or desirable about a mama's boy. A man should love his mother, and his mother should love him equally, if not more, but this is not what we are talking about here. A mama's boy is one who has an unhealthy relationship with his mother and himself. He is tied to her hips and trust me, ladies, when I say this, there is no space for you in that equation.

Get in a relationship with a mama's boy, and you will find yourself in the land of perpetual unhappiness. The sad part about it all is that the mothers are usually overbearing and you will be their biggest competition. They will go the extra mile to get you out of the picture because, in their eyes, you are never good enough. Thank God for all the mothers in the world who have a healthy relationship with their adult sons.

I have compiled a list of reasons why you shouldn't date a mama's boy.

- His mother will always be his number one priority.
- His mother will control his life.
- His mother will try to control your life.
- You will feel as though you got married to him and his mother.

- He will never be independent; to her, he is a baby who needs her. And he sees nothing wrong with that.
- His mother will be his confidant. She will hear about important things before you.
- He believes anything his mother tells him.
- She will always have the final say.
- He will continuously compare you to her.
- Nothing you do will ever be good enough if it is not done in the same way his mother does it.
- You will have to compete with her for his affection.
- He will take her side over yours.
- He will always want to have his way, and whenever he doesn't get it, he will throw a tantrum.

Can you live a happy life and have a happy marriage if your husband is like the boy described above?

# CHAPTER EIGHT

# THE KIND OF MAN YOU SHOULD MARRY

## LEADER, PROTECTOR, PROVIDER

Ladies, there is no doubt that we all have different preferences when it comes to the men we date and the men we wish to marry. As many of you know, preferences sometimes change as we get older. A man's physical appearance won't significantly make or break your life. Because of that, I am not here to talk about the cherry on the cake. I am here to talk about the characteristics of the man you should marry. You can figure out the rest whether you want him black, white, slim, or athletic. Your preferences are your choices, and no one's business.

When you decide to allow a man to court you, there are three main elements you should look for in that man. Make sure that this man is a Leader, A Protector, and A Provider. Everything you will ever want in a man apart from looks falls under one of these three categories. Do You desire a spiritual man? Well, that falls under leadership. Do You want a man who will please you sexually? That falls under the category of A Provider. A Provider aims to please not just financially but physically as well. Do you desire a faithful man, a man who cares about your heart? That right there falls under Protection. A man who protects won't just protect you physically; he will protect you emotionally and spiritually as well.

## MARRY A LEADER

The biggest problem with the world today is not with its political leaders. The biggest problem with the world begins in the family. The family is the foundation, the backbone of society. When a family unit is broken, a nation is broken, because this family produces children with messed up worldviews who later raise havoc in society. Most husbands and men, in general, don't realize that God has ordained them to be leaders. Some men know that they are called by God to be leaders in the home, but they don't know how to lead. Other men just don't want to lead. They want to be feminine, and so they transfer the role of leadership over to the women.

Now I love men. I admire men, and my greatest desire is to see men rise to their full potential and walk into their God-ordained role as leaders. Here are some of the reasons why most men fail to lead:

- They did not have a father who led.
- They didn't have any role models of men who lead.
- They have never been taught how to be a leader.
- Some men are simply lazy and want to relinquish the role of leadership over to their wives.
- Some men were manipulated by women, not to lead.

None of these excuses are valid. There is no reason why a man shouldn't be the leader of the home and family.

## HOW DOES A MAN WALK IN HIS ROLE AS LEADER?

He leads by loving. **A husband's leadership must be rooted in love.** Everything he says or does must be governed by this principle. **A man can be strong and brave and still be loving.** I have seen hunters and wrestling champions lead their wives and children with love like there was no tomorrow. I have seen front line military men lead their wives in love. Why? Because they knew how to lead.

He leads by Initiating and Decision Making. A man who leads by love will always make the first move. From the beginning of the courtship, he will pursue you, propose to you and set a wedding date. He will be the main instigator. He will initiate, and as a woman, you will respond. The perfect example of this is with God and mankind. 1 John 4:19 tells us, "We love Him because He first loved us." God was the initiator. We grow to love Him because He loves us first. Ladies, if a man loves you, he will be the initiator in the courtship and even after you are married.

A man who leads in decision making is a man who leads in all the other areas. If a man can lovingly lead his wife and do the initiating, it will be so easy for him to lead by decision making. Every woman will devotedly follow the decisions of a man she trusts.

He leads by example. This one is so simple, I don't have to go into great detail. Your husband will set the tone in the relationship by first leading by example. He will respect you; he will be an example in love, kindness, integrity, and truth. And as a woman of virtue, you will follow and give him in greater proportions all that he has given you.

I could go on for hours about several areas in which a man should take the lead, but because of time, I will stop here. A man who leads will also lead to reconciling. Every relationship has conflicts, but a man who leads won't display these behaviors:

- Explode in Anger whenever a conflict arises.
- Go away to pout whenever you disagree with him.
- Harden his heart or hold resentment.
- Gives you the silent treatment.
- Slams the door and breaks things.

A man who leads will walk in humility and tries to reconcile the union. He will take the lead and call you, come to seek you to restore that which is broken.

## MARRY A PROTECTOR

*Marry a Protector: Husbands, love your wives and do not be harsh with them.* Colossians 3:19 NIV

*Husbands, in the same way be considerate as you live with your wives, and treat them with respect as the weaker partner and as heirs with you of the gracious gift of life, so that nothing will hinder your prayers.*
1 Peter 3:7 NIV

Some people will argue that Christianity view women as inferior beings, but it is quite the opposite. God loves his daughters; He knows that He created us different from men. He gave his sons special instructions on how to treat us. A man who is in union with God will know that God has called him to protect his wife and children. We as women are capable of taking care of ourselves, it's not always easy, but many of us have. Now due to how differently we were made, our difference in abilities and strength, God has designated husbands to be protectors of their wives and family.

My Grandmother was a woman of strength, while my grandfather was very soft-spoken. However, he was the chief protector in the home. He slept at the end of the bed each night, just in case there was a break-in. He had his machete next to the bed always. No doubt, if he had a gun that would be right next to his bed, but he didn't have one. He was brave and ready to protect his wife and family. Whenever someone would say mean things about my grandma or ask him why he chose to marry such a witch, my grandfather was her chief defender. He protected her integrity by not speaking negativity about her or allowing people to plant negative things in his mind. Oh, oh, I wish to marry a man like my grandfather. A perfect example of this in today's modern world is Prince Harry; he is willing to do the unthinkable to protect his wife and son. He did all he could to ensure his wife doesn't suffer the same fate as his mother.

God designed men mentally, physically, and emotionally for the role of protector. Women can be fiery tongued; we will say a lot of hurtful things. We will act tough but put us in battle, and we crumble in fear. Ladies, this is the reason why we must marry a godly man who protects. God always gives the business of fighting to men. If we go back and search the Bible, we will see that God always commands the men to protect the nation. As mighty warriors, they never backed down. Men on the Titanic made sure the women and children were safe while they went down with the ship. Manliness has always been - associated with a willingness to be the hero and protector — woe to the nation who sends its women to fight.

In today's world, women are looked down on when they expect men to protect them. Feminism tells women to stand up for themselves, to fend for themselves, and the list goes on. Feminism is a weapon of darkness to breakdown the family unit. Deeply embedded in feminism is a spirit of antichrist.

Not all women desire to be men; I know I don't. I believe that most of you reading this book have the same mindset as myself. I love traditional values. I respect the Biblical standards laid out by my Creator. I want a man who will protect my children and me, not only from physical dangers but from emotional and spiritual threats as well. I want a man who will ensure that I don't become a man by becoming a more manlier version of myself. I am feminine, and I want to remain a woman, Loving, kind, and tenderhearted.

Ladies, you also have to make sure that you are marrying a man who protects you from his animalistic nature. He has to watch his anger and his outburst. Otherwise, you won't feel safe around him. That is the reason why God encouraged them to be gentle towards us as the weaker vessel.

If you desire a protector, marry a protector and don't settle for a man who isn't. It is okay if a man isn't a protector. It just means he isn't the man for you. At the end of the day, everyone has freedom of choice, and so do you, my sister in love. Please note that an abusive man is not a protector, and a true protector is not an abuser.

## MARRY A PROVIDER

Marry A Provider: When it comes to the Bible, there is no confusion on who should be the primary breadwinner in the home, Just like there is no confusion on who the primary homemaker should be. Men and women alike must know their mission to live a happy and productive life. A man's mission is to be a capable provider. Over the years, I have come to realize that some modern men don't have a problem leading, but they have a problem providing. A big reason for this is because people have become materialistic. Money has become their god. They don't fully trust the true God in the area of finances. God is the ultimate source, and their job is just a resource. When husbands begin to trust God again, they won't have a problem being a provider.

Apostle Paul clearly warns Christian men that if they don't provide for their family (immediate household), they have denied the faith and is worst than an infidel.

God has called men to provide, and if a wife steps up to join her husband to provide financially, that man ought to rejoice and not feel entitled. I love to make money, and I am going to make money doing what I love, and I will spend some of the money I earn in the home on my husband and children. I will do that because I am a virtuous woman. However, this does not take away from the fact that God has given men the role to be the primary bread winner in the home.

A godly man understands that a call to marriage is a call to provide for his wife and children. A righteous man will not stay home and play video games while his wife and children suffer. A godly husband will not be comfortable knowing that his wife is working two jobs to make ends meet while he watches her break down mentally and emotionally. I am not going to use my words lightly in this chapter. A man who doesn't do his very best to try and provide for his family is not worthy of being called a husband much less a Christian.

Recently I spoke with a woman who has been married for several years. Her husband stayed home playing video games all day while she went out to work. He never stood up to be man enough to provide for her and their children.

The bills piled up as the children got older, and her job alone couldn't cut it. Fed up, she decided to step out of the marriage and sleep with other men to get money to take care of the kids and pay the bills. When she came home with the money from the other men, her husband partook of the groceries too. Ladies, it is madness to take care of a grown man, he is not your son, he is a man.

Some men can't stay home with a baby for a day. They complain that it is too hard. They can't do it for a day, yet they expect you to work difficult jobs outside the home, have four kids, take care of those kids, while servicing them and keeping the home clean.

Ladies, do yourself a favor and get yourself a husband who provides. And that doesn't mean you won't work. If you want to it should be your choice but nothing should be a bigger priority than taking care of your husband and children. That is our primary role. Be a wife and a mother, and let your husband be the man. Real men provide, and real women appreciate it.

CHAPTER NINE

# LET'S HAVE COFFEE

Hello Ladies, we are almost at the end of the book, and I figured it was full time for us to have some coffee. The purpose of this book is basically to teach you how to value yourself more so that you can end up with a true Godly Man who leads, protect, and provides. Over the years, I have come to realize that women choose low-quality men because of low self-esteem. Some women also find themselves in marriages where the man treats them like a doormat instead of a queen. I don't want that for any of you ladies because there is nothing ordinary about you. You are phenomenal.

Recently I crossed path with a very beautiful lady, prior to her getting married. She and her husband agree to foot the bills fifty-fifty. It was never a problem for her at the time because she had a great job with lots of benefits. Unfortunately, several years into the marriage she lost her job and was unemployed for several months. She had to use the little money she had saved to cover her half of the bills. During this time, her husband didn't even bother to offer a helping hand. Finally, she found a job that paid way less than she made before. Not to mention her husband's salary is triple her income. In spite of that dynamic he refused to be the main provider.

A true husband with a sacrificial heart of love wouldn't feel comfortable to know that he is living in luxury while his wife is drowning in debt, no fault of hers.

A True Provider doesn't ask you to enter into some 50/50 agreement before marriage. A Roommate does that, not a husband. I remember when I shared an apartment with two other persons. Each month all three of us would split the rent, the electric, and the internet right down the middle. We were all comfortable with that arrangement. I didn't wake up and cook for them; they didn't wake up and cook for me. We all took turns cleaning the bathroom, the kitchen, and the living room. When outside was dirty, we all shared in the work. It was an arrangement but it was fine because we were housemates, and that was all there was to it.

As a woman, when you enter into some fifty-fifty arrangement before marriage, you are simply telling yourself that you don't value anything and that your role as a woman and a wife is not important. I don't believe in this whole feminism movement. It's not God's best for woman and it's not God's best for real men.

I am not saying women are more important than men, and I am not saying men are more important than women. I am simply saying that the role of a man in the marriage is different from the role of a woman. According to God, the primary roles of a husband is to lead, protect and provide. The roles of a wife are many. A godly wife should provide companionship for her husband. God gave Eve to Adam so that he wouldn't have to be alone. The woman was created for the man and not the other way around. My next book will be focused on how women can become better wives. Moving on to number two, a wife should love her husband always, and out of this love freely gives herself to him.

A wife should respect her husband. The Greek word Paul uses in Ephesians 5:33 when he mentions this kind of respect is "phobetai," which means to have a profound measure of reverence/respect. A wife should help her husband. There are multitudes of ways in which we can do this ladies. We can help our husband in providing good counsel and so forth. I am going to touch back on this point later on down in this chapter but let us continue for now.

A Christian wife should be completely devoted to her husband, body and soul. We can show our devotion by being faithful to our marriage vows, caring for our husband's sexual and emotional needs. We can be devoted to his calling by helping him to become the man God has called him to be.

We are also called to have self-respect as Christian wives in and out of the marriage. When we walk with dignity and have ethical conduct, other people will respect our husband because of this. We also need to have respect for our selves in the marriage. How do we carry this out? Let me give you the answer. We are supposed to expect proper treatment from our husband. We ought to expect love, protection, and provision. It is never okay for our husbands to abuse us. When we see abuse as normal, we have refused to walk in self-respect. Ephesians 5:28-29 encourages husbands to love their wives as their own bodies. Why? Because he who loves his wife loves himself. A husband ought to love and cherish his bride just like he would love and cherish himself.

Christian wives should also take care of their homes, not to mention a lot of women are mothers as well. Motherhood carries its own set of roles. When you become a mother, you won't just have the responsibility of caring for your husband; you will also have to nurture and care for your children.

I went into the roles of a woman to show you that they are far different from the roles of a man. Now let me ask you a question. Does this mean that a husband should not change a diaper or wash the dishes if you are not feeling well? I bet you are going to say he should because you are unable to and need his help. I bet if the man didn't help you with your role in your time of need, you would say he is selfish and unkind. Let that sink in for a moment.

Being a Christian wife doesn't mean you can't work outside of the home. There are Christian wives and mothers with jobs. I must admit some are overdoing it. They have neglected their primary role chasing after the dollars while their husbands are seeking companionship in the arms of another and their children are being raised by videos games and television. So yes, a woman can work outside of the home but it shouldn't be to the point where she has neglected her primary role. There are several ways wherein a woman can make money and still have a lot of time for her husband and children. She could work from home, teach via the internet, have an online business, etc.

I want you to read the following passage of scripture. She is the Proverbs 31 woman. May we become her and may we raise her.

## Proverbs 31:10-31

[10] [a]Who can find a virtuous and capable wife?
  She is more precious than rubies.
[11] Her husband can trust her,
  and she will greatly enrich his life.
[12] She brings him good, not harm,
  all the days of her life.

[13] She finds wool and flax
  and busily spins it.
[14] She is like a merchant's ship,
  bringing her food from afar.
[15] She gets up before dawn to prepare breakfast for her household
  and plan the day's work for her servant girls.

[16] She goes to inspect a field and buys it;
  with her earnings she plants a vineyard.
[17] She is energetic and strong,
  a hard worker.
[18] She makes sure her dealings are profitable;
  her lamp burns late into the night.

[19] Her hands are busy spinning thread,
  her fingers twisting fiber.
[20] She extends a helping hand to the poor

and opens her arms to the needy.
[21] She has no fear of winter for her household,
for everyone has warm[b] clothes.

[22] She makes her own bedspreads.
She dresses in fine linen and purple gowns.
[23] Her husband is well known at the city gates,
where he sits with the other civic leaders.
[24] She makes belted linen garments
and sashes to sell to the merchants.

[25] She is clothed with strength and dignity,
and she laughs without fear of the future.
[26] When she speaks, her words are wise,
and she gives instructions with kindness.
[27] She carefully watches everything in her household
and suffers nothing from laziness.

[28] Her children stand and bless her.
Her husband praises her:
[29] "There are many virtuous and capable women in the world,
but you surpass them all!"

[30] Charm is deceptive, and beauty does not last;
but a woman who fears the Lord will be greatly praised.
[31] Reward her for all she has done.
Let her deeds publicly declare her praise.

## THE WEDDING VOWS

"_____, wilt thou have this man to be thy wedded husband to live together after God's ordinance in the Holy Estate of matrimony? Wilt thou love him? Comfort him, honor and keep him, in sickness and in health, and forsaking all others keep thee only unto him as long as you both shall live?"

"In the name of God, I, _____, take you, _____, to be my husband, to have and to hold from this day forward, for better, for worse, for richer, for poorer, in sickness and health, to love and to cherish, until we are parted by death. This is my solemn vow."

Ladies, the above are traditional Christian wedding vows. I want to point out that marriage is not like a driver's license. It is not something you can have the option to renew every five years and don't if you don't feel like it. Marriage is for better or for worst. While it is not the duty of the wife to carry the financial burden of her household or even to split the bills fifty-fifty, as godly women, if we have a job or a business that earns income, we can help our husband with the financial load if he is not able to.

During a tough economy, some husband's may find it difficult to get work. Should a wife not assist her husband or pay for the children to go to private school if she has the means? If a wife can, she absolutely should. If you are a wife making way more than your husband, and you wish to get him a car for Christmas or invest in real estate, go ahead and do so. Marriage is not a secular business arrangement and any money you spend in marriage, whether you spend it on your husband or children, you are still benefiting in the end. It is an investment in an institution that cannot and will not fail if both people are surrendered to God.

This book is not a gold digging book. It is a book that is encouraging you to stay away from dusty men who bails on their financial responsibility as a husband and father. It is not fair for us as women to struggle and carry the financial burden of the home while having babies, raising children, taking care of our husbands, the home and ourselves. A husband who is financially able to lead, protect, and provide for his family and refuse to do so is selfish and very troubling. But to those husbands who have the heart and the desire and is falling short along the way, may we be like the proverbs thirty-one woman and help out where we can. That is another way in which we can be a helpmate to our husbands.

Whatever belongs to you belongs to your husband, and whatever belongs to your husband belongs to you. If your husband is sick and can't pay the bill for two months and you can, by all means, pay it. Think back to my discussion about my grandparent's relationship in chapter three. While my grandma didn't work outside of the home, she was a seamstress. Just like The Proverbs 31 woman, she would make clothes, curtains, and bedding and sell it to people near and far. In addition to that, she sold eggs from the many chickens we had. She also made money selling cows and goats. She didn't physically care for them herself, my grandpa did, but many of them belonged to her. Even though my grandfather worked and provided, there were several times when he was out of money, but he didn't have to worry about it. Grandma would always give him money whenever he ran short. I know that many times she was simply giving him back money from what he gave her in the past. But I also know that some of the money he used to go to doctor or get new clothing was from the money my grandma got from her business.

She didn't complain or refuse to help him out. Oh no, she was happy and proud to do that. That was her husband, the bone of her bone and the flesh of her flesh. I am certain that she wouldn't have helped him out if he wasn't a provider. And I am also certain that she wouldn't be eager to help him if they had some stupid 50/50 arrangement going on. They were each other's heartbeat and they were willing to love and sacrifice for each other body and soul.

"When A Man Leads, Protects and Provides a woman will respond in love and do anything for that man." Ann-Marie Graham

I hope you enjoyed the coffee Beloved.

# CHAPTER TEN

# BECOME THE WOMAN

Ladies, do you desire a masculine man who will lead, protect, and provide for you? Do you want him to see you as his treasure? Do you want him to love and cherish you for life? Well, if that is your desire, you must not only have the qualities of a feminine woman. You must become the feminine woman.

A masculine man cannot resist a feminine woman. He desires and adores her. The masculine energy is attracted to feminine energy like a magnet to metal. This little book is unlike any other because I am not teaching you how to be fake or go out of your way to buy expensive clothing and jewelry. No, I am guiding you to become feminine from within, how to harness the feminine energy ingrained in you by the Creator. Some of the most feminine woman in the world today don't even wear Gucci or Prada. Becoming feminine is something that first happens within us, not outside.

As a young woman growing up, I was the leader, the alpha female, because that is who my mother raised me to be. I remember even hating the idea of flowers. My ex brought me flowers once, and I thought it was a waste of money. As I shed away old patterns of beliefs, I have come to appreciate flowers. I didn't force it to happen; no one told me that I should love flowers; it just happened. I let go of the belief that I was a strong woman who leads, and this certainly doesn't mean I have no strength. I am not a strong masculine woman, but I am a woman of strength, who knows how to appropriate her energy.

I let go of every belief that said I could do it all by myself. As I let go of these old patterns of consciousness, I started becoming more feminine from within. I even went out and got fresh flowers for my home, and this is a practice that I will continue to do. I can't begin to tell you about the effects those flowers had on my mood and my home. But that will be for a blog on my website at www.upfromthedust.org.

This chapter is your guide to becoming and attracting the masculine man.

## VULNERABILITY

Femininity is about vulnerability, taking off that masculine mask that many of us women put on each day. The disguise that we often put on to feel good about ourselves. The veil that says I am dominant and powerful, I don't need a man. I can do it all alone. Being vulnerable is about surrendering to our Creator and the feminine energy he placed within. Surrendering to the feminine energy is not an easy task today because it is often looked down upon. It is labeled as weak and lazy. But the truth is the feminine energy is courageous. It takes courage to have and give birth to a child. It takes courage to make sure everyone in the home is happy when so many things are falling apart.

To become a feminine woman, you have to surrender to life and all that it entails fully. You have to learn to feel. You have to learn to experience pleasure, feel pain, grieve, express your emotions. This is what surrendering to life means. It means showing up as your authentic self, whatever your state of consciousness, and not putting on a mask that is politically correct and pleasing to the crowd.

In the mind of a masculine man, if you are not vulnerable, you don't need him. A masculine man wants to know that you need him, and believe me when I say this, nothing is wrong with that. If the vulnerability is not there, a dominant man will just put you in the category of one of the many women he sleeps with and then dumps. He won't see you as the prize or treasure that he wants to spend forever with. A dominant man doesn't want to debate with the men at work and come home to a woman who is captain of the debate team. He wants to go home to his safe place. A safe place for him is vulnerability and tenderness.

## GETTING RID OF THE TOXIC

To become a feminine woman, you have to let go of all the toxicity taught to you by society, family members, and even yourself. You have to let go of old limiting beliefs and embrace new life-giving ideas. Embrace the truth given to you by The Creator; you are an extension of the man. You are his helpmate. Society today tells us that this is a bad thing, but that is far from the truth. Being a helpmate to a man is a significant role, a great compliment. A lot of men are great and powerful today because they had wonderful mothers and great wives.

Ladies, sometimes you will need a Life Coach to help you heal and get over these limiting beliefs, don't be afraid to seek one out. Most times, we as women have been so badly hurt to the point where we put up this masculine barrier to protect ourselves. While masculine energy is sometimes needed, it should never be our most dominant energy because we aren't a man. Our true strength should come from our femininity and not from masculinity.

## TIPS TO BECOME MORE FEMININE

## YOUR HYGIENE

Make sure that you are clean, soft, and fresh. I would encourage you to shower or take a bath in the mornings and at night. Groom your nails and neatly comb your hair. Groom, your pubic hair, don't allow them to grow wild.

## CLOTHING

Wear clothes that compliment your body type. They don't have to be from a top designer or a designer at all. Just make sure they are clean, elegant, and classy. Do not dress cheap and trashy. Wear a suitable feminine shoes that compliment your outfit.

# BODY

Ladies I am not telling you to become a size six, I am not a size six either. However, I do take care of my body, and that is what I am encouraging you to do. Let go of the junk food, maintain a healthy diet, drink lots of water, sign up to the gym, or take daily walks.

# UNDERWEAR

Ladies, even if you are not married as yet, get some good underwear. Let go of underwear's that have lived way past their expiration date. Get some with lace, you will love them and when you get married, your husband will love them too.

# POSTURE

This won't cost you a dime, and when you get older, your body will thank you for it. Having a proper posture will help you to look more feminine. A good posture has a direct effect on your mood as well as on the way others see you. A masculine man is attracted to a woman with proper posture. A correct posture is ladylike.

# PERFUME

Wear a delicate flowery scented fragrance or something exotic and mild. Nothing too strong as that sends off a masculine vibe. A man cannot resist a woman who smells like happiness.

## DO NOT GOSSIP

Ladies, if you want to attract a masculine man, you cannot be a gossiper. A dominant man sees a gossiper as a total waste of time. If you are, he won't see you as his prize or the mother of his future children. Remember that a dominant man knows what he wants and who he wants, and you have to become the woman he wants.

## SENSE OF HUMOR

A man loves a woman he can relax with and have a good time with now and again. So ladies, don't be afraid to be playful, but don't go overboard to the point where you become sarcastic.

## BE YOURSELF

Express your own unique version of feminine energy. What this mean is that you have to come to the place where you find out what your own feminine expression looks like. It involves living from your truth and following your unique style. That is why I only covered the basics in this chapter. I didn't tell you to wear red lipstick or wear only a tightly fitted dress because that is not everyone's style. Femininity to you may be wearing lip-gloss instead of red lipstick. It may even mean wearing pink lipstick. There aren't any rules ladies, there are just guidelines. We all have feminine energy, and I desire that we will express higher feminine energy. My prayer is that we will embrace life, be vulnerable, and stop wearing the pants in the relationship. Be the woman. Let loose your feminine energy.

## SURRENDER TO EMOTIONAL INTIMACY

Give a genuine smile: I remember once I went to see a doctor, and the first thing I greeted him with was a kind, beautiful, and genuine smile. I wasn't trying to flirt with my doctor, but his reaction was priceless. He said, "My day has been crazy, but you have just made my day with that smile. I bet you change the life of everyone you meet." And I just smiled again and said, "Yes, I do." Giving a man a genuine smile with eye contact is a great way to release your feminine energy.

Ladies, you also have to learn how to appreciate your man and don't be afraid to show him kindness. You were born to nurture and to love. Don't be mean, loud, and boisterous. Most importantly, ladies don't be pretentious.

Last but not least, love yourself, respect yourself, be kind to yourself. Don't be afraid to spoil you. You can't expect a man to treat you like a princess when you treat yourself like a doormat.

Give yourself the princess experience and a man will make you his queen.

# CHAPTER ELEVEN

# AFFIRMATIVE PRAYER TO ATTRACT A MUSCULINE HUSBAND

15 Minutes Nightly Prayer And Visualization Treatment

Before you fall asleep at night, I want you to pray the prayer below.

After which I want you to lay in bed and visualize your husband in your life. Imagine that you are already married, imagine your nightly routine with your husband. Imagine how you will make him feel and how he will make you feel. Feel the emotions of happiness that come along with having this man in your life.

After your visualization treatment, thank God for your husband, close your eyes, and fall asleep.

Father I know that you always hear me, Thank you for hearing me. I am your Daughter, thank you for creating me. In you, all men and women live and move and have their being. We are all your sons and daughter and you know each and every one of us. I know God that you have A Husband, A Leader, A Protector and A Provider waiting to love and cherish me. I will contribute to his life and help him to fulfill his purpose and destiny here on this earth. I know too that he can and will help me to fulfill my purpose and destiny. Thank you that this man loves me for who I am and I love him for who he is and we are not trying to change each other. There is mutual love, peace and benefit in our union.

Father I thank you that there is only one Consciousness and that is God consciousness. I know this man in God consciousness and he knows me in God consciousness. I now unite with my husband in my heart and spirit. As a feminine woman I unite and compliment his role as a masculine man. Thank You God that I see You in him and he sees You in me. Thank You Father that I will meet this man and he will pursue me and treat me like the treasure and gift that I am. Thank you, Father, that these words that goes from my mouth have gone forth to accomplish what I say in Jesus name Amen.

Affirmative Prayer composed By Ann-Marie Graham

# MEET ANN-MARIE GRAHAM

**I HELP WOMEN GO FROM ORDINARY TO PHENOMENAL!**

**FOLLOW OUR BLOG @** **WWW.UPFROMTHEDUST.ORG**

*I was born in a one-room wooden structure in the serene countryside of Westmoreland, Jamaica. On November 9th, 1990, I breathe my first breath into a family of dysfunction and a generation crippled by limiting beliefs. My father was never around to show me how a man is supposed to treat a woman. My mother couldn't teach me how to become a phenomenal woman because she was programmed to being a strong black woman.*

*As a child growing up, I suffered from low self-esteem. Still, very few people would realize as I was a professional at hiding behind a mask called "A Smile." My childhood was crippled by verbal, emotional, and sometimes physical abuse. Ill health became a crutch, I enjoyed it when I was sick because I thought I would somehow get a little affection, some words of affirmation which I craved so much but my desire was never satisfied.*

*At eighteen years old, I got married to the first man that told me he loves me and gave me some affection. His Words to me were like the* oasis in the desert. But my minute of happiness was cut short when he told me three months into our marriage that he didn't love me. He said, "I remember the first day I saw you, there was this light on you and I knew I had to marry you. I marry you for the light but Ann-Marie I do not love you."

Those words cut like a knife, but I did try to stay and make my marriage work. But ever so often, when I was alone, I would dream and see myself as a woman who is loved and who gives love unconditionally. I would see this woman in me. I would see myself as a woman who inspires and touch other girls and women to pursue their purpose and become phenomenal.

Then one night, he told me that we aren't right for each other. He told me how broken I was and mocked my childhood. I remember telling him that I know I am broken, but I want a man who was willing to soothe my pain and kiss my scars. Though I didn't say anything further to him that night, I promised myself that the next time he told me he didn't love me and didn't want to be with me, I would respect myself enough to walk away.

March of 2009, just five months after marriage, I packed my bags and kissed heartbreak goodbye.

It wasn't easy; the struggle steadily grew more real. Anxiety was my daily companion since the tender age of fourteen, but when I walked out of that marriage, depression became a permanent tenant. On a few different occasions, she would bring along her cousin's suicidal thoughts and pessimism, unwelcomed guests in my heart. Not to mention the *loneliness of not having a support unit, coupled with the dire financial situation, poverty, and worst of all, a lack of opportunity.*

*Nothing caused me more considerable distress than being an A Player living a B life. I wanted the opportunity of self-expression, but I got none until...*

*I Found God; I found people who do the same work that I do now, and they helped me to learn the secret of God, the mystery of me, and the Language of the world.*

*My childhood and early life was nothing to be celebrated. It was instead something to heal from. Today I am not only healed, but I am healing others. I tapped into my inherent phenomenal nature and cultivated the gifts and talents given to me by God.*

*I once asked The Purpose Giver the reason for my existence, and His gentle, still small voice said, "Ann-Marie, your purpose is to help people find their purpose." I see myself as a farmer who heals. I don't cultivate crops; I cultivate people. I am an Inner Gardener. I build, and I plant the positive, and I root up, pull down, and tear down the negative. I am A Prophetess Ordained By God for such a time as this.*

*Along my journey, I have discovered two things; all women are born extraordinary and phenomenal; however, our family, our culture, the media, and society sometimes program us to be ordinary. The second thing I have learned is that we all can cultivate the qualities that will make us unforgettable.*

*I am a woman of unlimited potential, who by choice, is creating a life by design through faith in God, focus, and a commitment to become* the best version of myself. I want to go down in history as the woman who rose from the dust to purpose, the woman who rises from the ashes to become a diamond, a mother of this generation, simply because she was born To Be. I am Ann-Marie Graham, a phenomenal, phenomenal woman that's me.

And Beloved Woman, I Want The Same For You!!

That is the reason why the Spirit led me to create Up From The Dust To A Life Of Purpose as well as The Phenomenal Woman Academy.

# OTHER BOOKS BY ANN-MARIE GRAHAM

## 30 Days To Your Best Life

*30 Days to your Best Life* is more than a fly by night solution to all your problems; it's a step-by-step guide to living the life you were meant to live in God's eyes.

Written in an easy-to-follow format by Ann-Marie Graham, an enigmatic minister and dynamic motivational speaker, this devotional journal walks you through three stages dubbed the Three E's:

*Expectation of faith*

*Expression of faith*

*Exploits of faith*

Each stage is an important building block for your faith. With each passing day, you will find your life's purpose, learn to embrace God's love, and exponentially grow your faith.

Take this 30-day journey. It just might be the most influential days of your life. Purchase via this link: 30 Days to Your Best Life Devotional

# God's Healing Promises

When many hear the term 'faith healing', they're immediately skeptical, yet, these same people rave about the pharmaceutical industry. That presents quite the quandary.

What does one do to overcome the doubt they feel about God and his ability to heal?

*God's Healing Promises* aims to marry your lingering doubts with God's healing powers. Using HIS words and the principles derived from them, this book will revolutionize your life, one transformational message at a time.

Immerse yourself in God's words, embrace the underlying messages, and let the lessons you learn transform your life, starve the disease of doubt and uncertainty, and allow God's healing grace to flow through you and through all that you do from this moment forward.

Feeding your faith is the key to starving the disease. Purchase via this link: God's Healing Promises

Made in the USA
San Bernardino, CA
15 February 2020